Sammy The Sloth

Written By
Thomas Conti

Illustrated By
Jonny hossain

This Book is dedicated to
our son Thomas Conti Jr.
-Love Mom and Dad

Hello everyone. I'm Ranger Sammy Sloth.
I'm here before sunrise at the park to open the
gate every morning.

Of course, I sleep at the gate to make it on time
daily. You see, as a sloth, I can be pretty slow at
times, but this is not a bad thing.

2

"No need to worry or be in a hurry." That is what I like to say. I take my time and do an excellent job with everything I do.

If it doesn't get done today, it will be finished tomorrow. "A rushed job is never well done." That is what father sloth always told me.

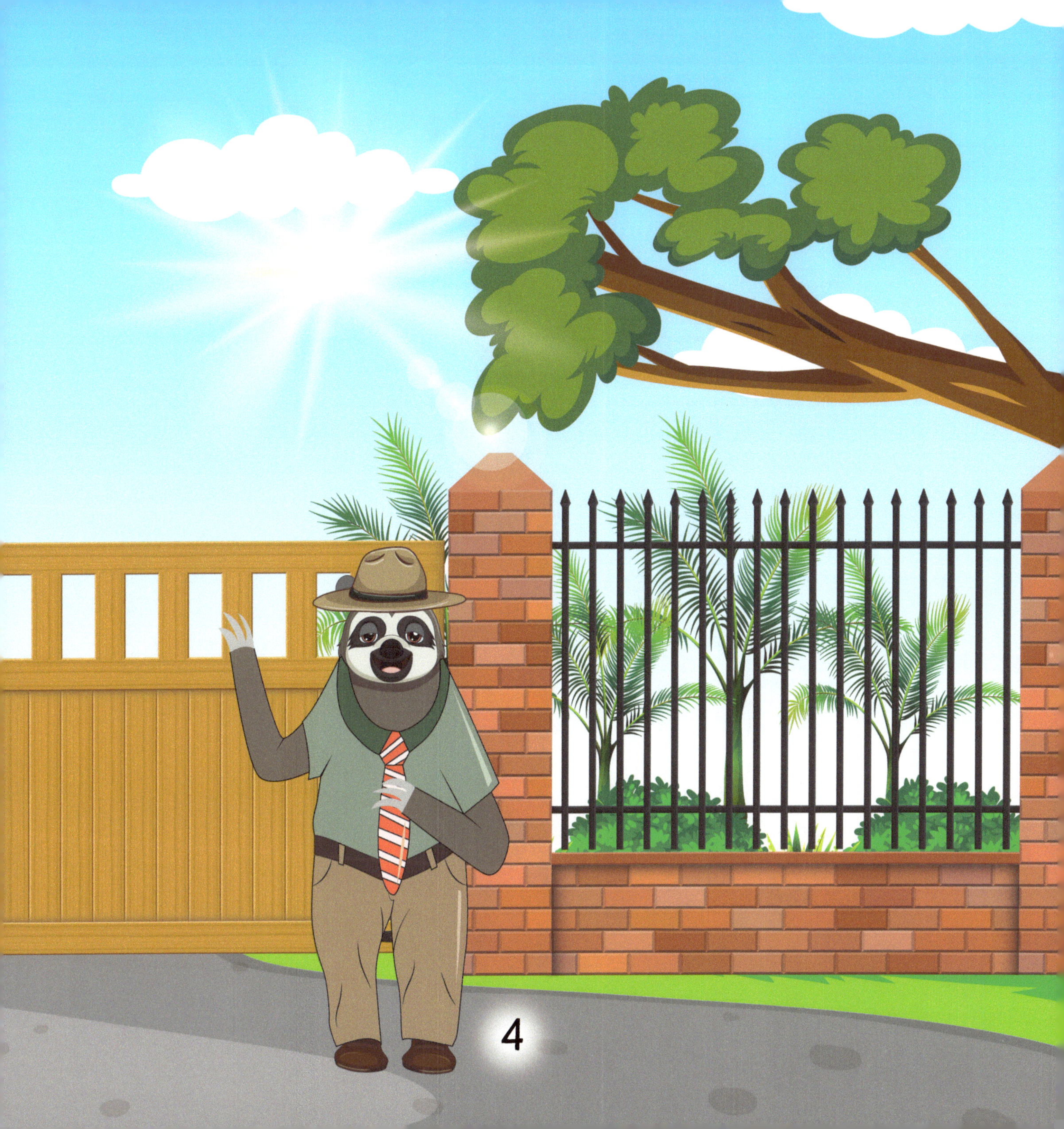

4

I will teach you the ways of the sloth if you would like. We love nature and are positive thinkers!

I'm a three-toed sloth.
One, Two, and Three toes on each arm.

6

My toes are hooked, so I can hang on branches with ease. On my days off, I hang in the trees.

Enough about me, though...
Now that the gate is open, we must start our day as park rangers!

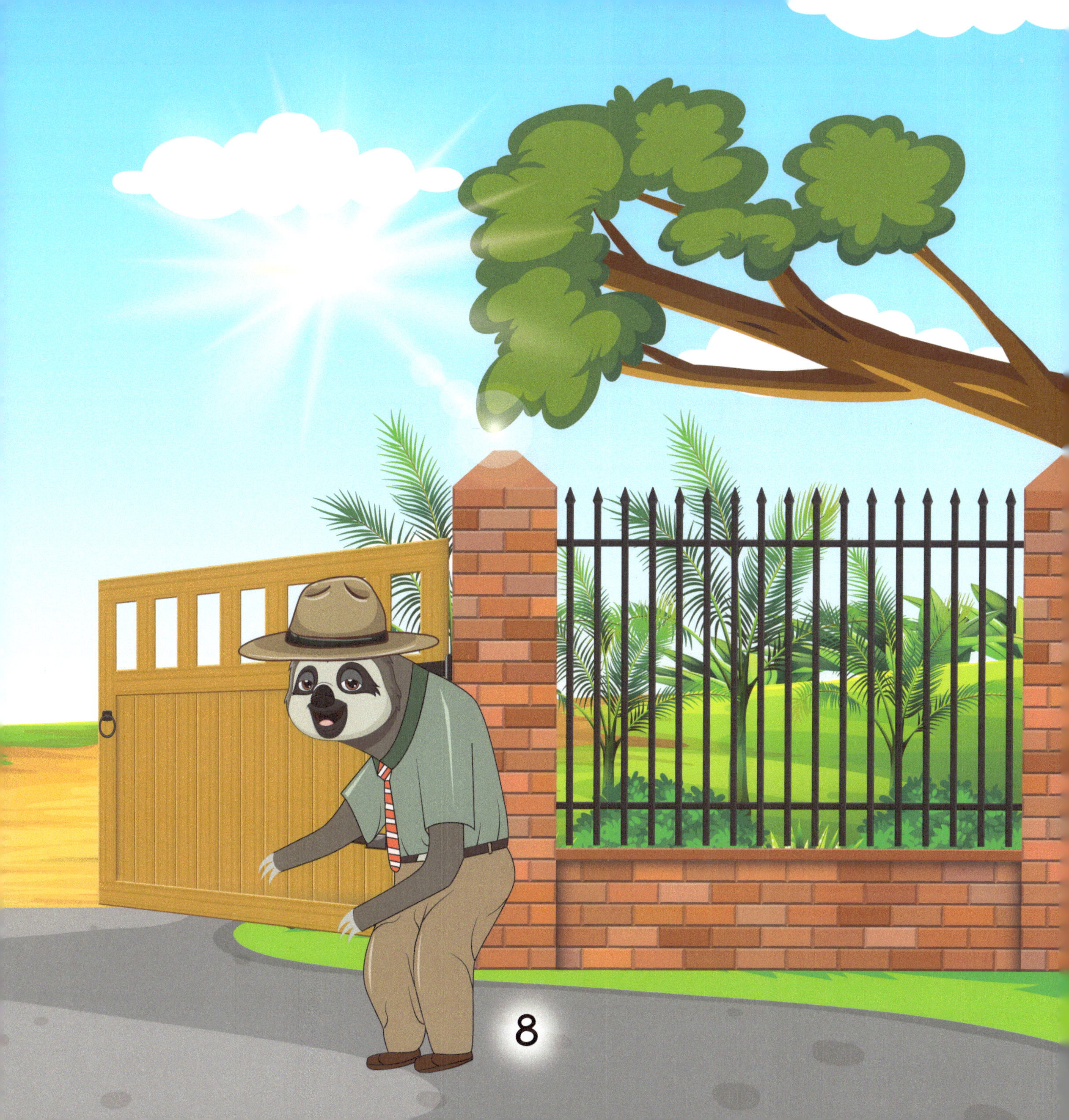

8

The first thing we do in the morning after opening
the main gate is patrol the park,
But we need to get you all your ranger badges and
gear.

Slowly... Let's walk this way now, everybody.
We must head over to the ranger station to get our
supplies.

Every ranger needs a badge to show that he or she is a real ranger. Make sure your badge is displayed proudly.

Next, everybody put on their boots to walk through the rough outdoors. Last, here is a map to help us find our way around the park.

MAP
12

It's time to patrol the park and the trails.
We get an off-road vehicle to drive along the trails
known as the SlothMobile.

The SlothMObile has many features that help sloth
rangers do their jobs better,
Everything a sloth ranger will need, the Slothmobile
provides, and more...

It has a megaphone, so I can make announcements
that can be heard from far away,
and lots of other ranger accessories for completing
park duties.

Rangers are responsible for removing invasive plants from the park. Removing invasive plants allow the local plants to grow strong.

Pruning vines and branches along the trails helps to keep the path clear. Cleared paths lead to fun and safe hiking for everyone!

16

Let's head down the Pine Tree trail looking for any blocked paths. It is our job to keep trails clear and safe.

There's a downed tree up ahead that must be re-moved. We will need to cut it up and roll the logs to the side.

18

Rangers have special training for using ranger equipment safely. We only use equipment that we are
trained to operate.

Luckily our SlothMobile has all the supplies we need
for removing trees. We cut the log into 1, 2, 3, 4, 5
pieces and roll them off the trail.

Now we can easily continue driving down the trail,
But keep an eye out for nature while on the trails.

The parks are filled with many amazing things.
There are beautiful sites to be seen and special
sounds to be heard in nature!

When we take our time and enjoy the outdoors,
We can notice things that may have been
overlooked.

22

An Eagle is seen soaring high above in the sky,
And a creek is heard babbling in the distance.

All our 5 senses our stimulated while out in nature.
Touch, taste, see, hear, and smell the great
outdoors!

Nature is such a wonderful and delightful gift,
And it is the job of a park ranger to keep nature
healthy!

One of our jobs is to help preserve and protect wildlife. Animals and plants rely on us to live longer and healthier lives.

Park rangers make sure people are not destroying the parks. Keeping the park clean of trash is a great way of helping nature!

25

26

Now that you learned the ways of the sloth,
It's up to you to keep nature safe and the parks
clean!

Be sure to respect nature and take your time to
enjoy the beautiful sites at the park!
I look forward to seeing you on our next adventure!

28